# DK Spot the

# Bug

## Tom Jackson

LONDON, NEW YORK, MUNICH,
MELBOURNE, AND DELHI

**DK LONDON**
**Senior Art Editor** Jacqui Swan
**Editor** Wendy Horobin
**Production Editor**
Francesca Wardell
**Production Controller** Alice Sykes
**Jacket Designer** Mark Cavanagh
**Managing Art Editor**
Michelle Baxter
**Managing Editor** Angeles Gavira
**Publisher** Sarah Larter
**Art Director** Philip Ormerod
**Associate Publishing Director**
Liz Wheeler
**Publishing Director**
Jonathan Metcalf

**DK DELHI**
**Designer** Konica Juneja
**Senior Art Editor** Anuj Sharma
**Senior Editor** Vineetha Mokkil
**Deputy Managing Art Editor**
Sudakshina Basu
**Managing Editor**
Rohan Sinha
**Senior DTP Designer**
Harish Aggarwal
**DTP Manager/CTS**
Balwant Singh
**Production Manager**
Pankaj Sharma
**Picture Researcher**
Ashwin Adimari

First published in 2013 by Dorling Kindersley Limited
80 Strand, London WC2R 0RL
Penguin Group (UK)

2 4 6 8 10 9 7 5 3
005 – 187705 – Apr/2013
Copyright © 2013 Dorling Kindersley Limited

A CIP catalogue record for this book is available from the British Library
ISBN 978-1-40936-677-5

Printed and bound in China
by South China Printing Company (Ltd)

Discover more at
**www.dk.com**

## Stickers

Once you have seen a bug, find its sticker at
the back of the book and add it to the page.

Seen it!

Seen it!

# Contents

**Plus over 100 stickers
at the back**

## Icons

♂ This symbol is used to show when a male bug
is pictured, if the female looks different.

Habitat – where
the bug lives

Food – what
the bug eats

Size of the
bug

# Identifying bugs

There are hundreds of different types of bugs living around you. Before you start to look, you need to know some simple rules to help you identify them.

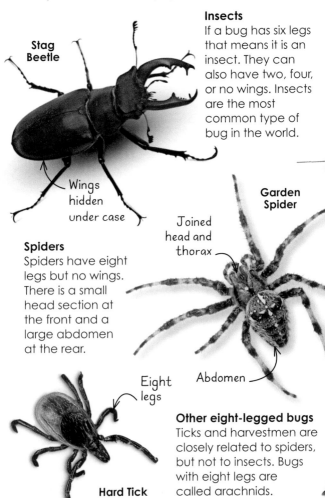

### Insects
If a bug has six legs that means it is an insect. They can also have two, four, or no wings. Insects are the most common type of bug in the world.

**Stag Beetle**

Wings hidden under case

### Spiders
Spiders have eight legs but no wings. There is a small head section at the front and a large abdomen at the rear.

**Garden Spider**

Joined head and thorax

Abdomen

Eight legs

**Hard Tick**

### Other eight-legged bugs
Ticks and harvestmen are closely related to spiders, but not to insects. Bugs with eight legs are called arachnids.

## Centipedes and millipedes

The names of these bugs suggest they have a hundred or even a thousand legs but neither has this many. The legs stick out from the side of the body, which is divided up into segments. It is easy to tell which is which – centipedes are long-legged and fast moving while millipedes are short-legged and slow.

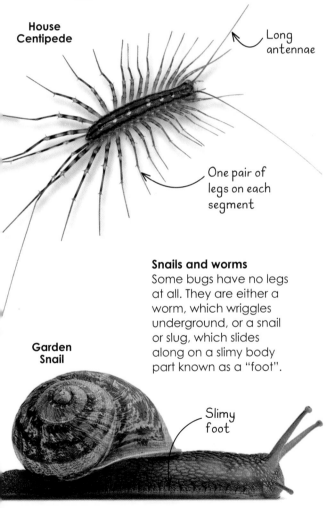

**House Centipede**

Long antennae

One pair of legs on each segment

### Snails and worms

Some bugs have no legs at all. They are either a worm, which wriggles underground, or a snail or slug, which slides along on a slimy body part known as a "foot".

**Garden Snail**

Slimy foot

# Bug bodies

Most of the bugs you find will be insects and spiders. If you get to know their different body parts, it will help you figure out which one is which.

### Insect body
The word "insect" comes from "in sections", and all adult insects have a body made up of three main sections. At the front is the head, in the middle is the thorax, and at the back is the abdomen.

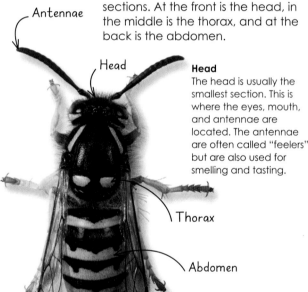

Antennae

Head

### Head
The head is usually the smallest section. This is where the eyes, mouth, and antennae are located. The antennae are often called "feelers" but are also used for smelling and tasting.

Thorax

Abdomen

Wings

### Abdomen
The abdomen is usually the largest section and contains most of the digestive system. If an insect has a stinger then it is at the tip of the abdomen.

### Thorax
The insect's wings (if it has them) and six legs are always attached to this middle section.

## Spider body

Like insects, spiders have a body split into sections, but they have two sections rather than three. The head and thorax are joined together. The second section is the abdomen.

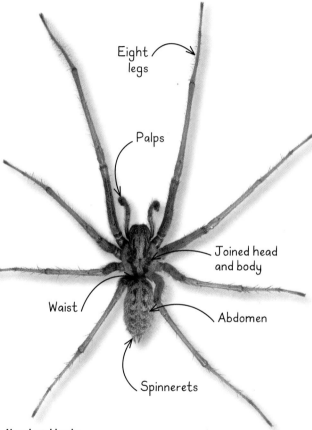

Eight legs

Palps

Joined head and body

Waist

Abdomen

Spinnerets

### Head and body

The legs are attached to the head and body section. Spiders don't have antennae, but they do have two palps – little arm-like structures on the front of the head. Spiders can have up to eight eyes.

### Abdomen

This section is divided from the head and body by a narrow "waist". A spider's silk organs, known as the spinnerets, are located at the tip of the abdomen.

# Where to look

You will not have any trouble finding bugs. They live almost everywhere – even in your home. Every bug has a favourite place to live or feed.

### Leafy shrubs
Many bugs eat plants, so you can always find some in a garden or park. Some will live on the stems, while others crawl around on the leaves or the ground beneath the plant.

### Wild flowers
The reason why some flowers are brightly coloured and smell sweetly is to attract flying bugs to them. The bugs come to the flower to drink its sweet nectar and nibble on pollen.

### Dark and damp
Bugs often like damp, dark places to live or hide in. Turn over logs or large stones and you'll find plenty of bugs. A cellar or garden shed is also a good place to find them.

### Ponds

There are many bugs that live in water. The best place to spot them is in a clear pond. Don't touch the water – it will scare them off. Just sit and watch carefully.

### Around lights

No one is sure why, but on warm summer nights bugs can be seen fluttering around lights. It might simply be because they confuse the light with the Moon, which some insects use for finding their way around.

### High fliers

Some flying insects, especially little flies and gnats, gather in groups (called swarms) above tall objects, such as fence posts, street lamps, or even people's heads!

# Food and feeding

Insects and spiders do not have jaws and teeth. Their mouths are made up of many small sections that are shaped according to what they feed on.

### Spider fangs
Spiders bite their prey with two poisonous fangs. They then pump chemicals into their victim's body, which turns it into goo. The spider sucks this up through its tube-shaped mouthparts.

### Chewing
Grasshoppers have mouthparts that are good for slicing and chewing up tough leaves.

### Sponge
A House Fly has spongey mouthparts that soak up juices and liquids that ooze from rotting meat.

### Sucking

Plant bugs suck the sap from stems through a needle-sharp mouthpart that is tucked under the body when not being used.

### Proboscis

Moths and butterflies drink liquid food – often nectar or fruit juices – and they use a straw-like mouthpart called a proboscis. This is coiled up when the insect is not feeding.

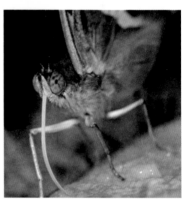

### Slicing

Ants' jaws slice easily through food, but are gentle enough to carry their young.

# A growing bug

Most of the pictures in this book are of adult bugs. They don't all start out like that. Many go through a process of change called metamorphosis.

### Complete change

A bug such as a fly or beetle begins life as a larva. The larva is basically an eating machine. Once it has had enough food it will change into the adult.

**Mating**
Males and females mate to create a new brood of flies.

**Egg**
The female fly lays tiny eggs near a good supply of food.

**Maggot**
The fly larva that hatches is called a maggot. It has no legs or proper eyes, and eats non-stop.

Pupa

**Adult**
The new adult emerges from its pupal case, and starts searching for a mate.

**Pupa**
Once it's big enough, the maggot's skin hardens into a thick case called a pupa. Inside, the bug changes into an adult before breaking out.

## Incomplete change

Other insects, such as plant bugs and grasshoppers, hatch out of their eggs as nymphs. Unlike a larva, the nymph looks like a small version of the adult form. While nymphs have six legs, they only grow wings when they become adults.

**Egg**
The female grasshopper lays eggs in soil.

**Nymph**
A tiny nymph hatches out and feeds.

**Adult**
The final instar is the adult, which has developed wings and can fly.

**Instars**
As the nymph grows, it sheds its skin. Each time it does this it forms a new, bigger version called an instar.

# Shedding skin

Bugs have a tough outer skin called an exoskeleton that supports their bodies. However, it does not stretch as the bug grows, so it must be shed, or moulted.

### Moulting process

Before an insect can moult, it grows a fresh skin under the old one. Then the outer one becomes unstuck from the rest of the body, dries out, and splits open. The insect pushes itself out of the old skin. It then puffs itself up with air to stretch out any wrinkles in the new, soft exoskeleton and waits for it to go hard.

### Skin cases

Sometimes the old exoskeleton falls off in flakes, but you may come across a whole case. The easiest ones to find are from the spiders living in your house. They moult in corners and other sheltered places. The biggest cases can be found in late summer and autumn.

# Useful words

**Abdomen**
The large rear section of an insect or spider body.

**Antennae**
The flexible "feelers" on the head of a bug, used for smell, touch, and taste.

**Crustacean**
An animal with jointed segments and limbs and a tough shell, such as a lobster or shrimp.

**Dormant**
Describes a bug that has become inactive because of the season or other changes in its environment.

**Exoskeleton**
The hard, protective outer case of an insect.

**Halteres**
The shrunken hind wings of some types of insect that help it balance while flying.

**Larva**
A young form of an insect that goes through a complete change of body shape to become an adult, for example, a caterpillar that changes into a butterfly.

**Maggot**
A fly larva, a small worm-like bug that lives in food waste.

**Metamorphosis**
The process that turns a young insect into an adult version. After several moults, the larva stops feeding and spins a protective outer case called a pupa. Inside the pupa, all the body organs break down and reassemble. The adult eventually chews or bursts its way out.

**Nymph**
A young insect that looks a lot like its final adult shape, but does not have wings.

**Ovipositor**
The egg-laying tube in the abdomen of a female insect. In ants and wasps this tube is used as a stinger.

**Palp**
The small arm-like structure in front of the mouth that spiders use for sensing or to hold food.

**Parasite**
An animal that grows or feeds on another species.

**Predator**
An animal that hunts and eats other animals.

**Prey**
An animal that is hunted by another for food.

**Spiderling**
A baby spider.

**Thorax**
The middle section of an insect's body to which the wings and legs are attached.

**Wing case**
A hard outer case that protects the hind wings.

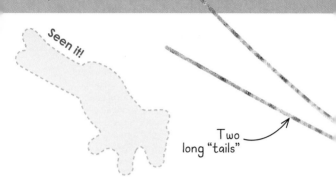

Seen it!

Two
long "tails"

# Pond Olive

This small mayfly can be
spotted around ponds and
riverbanks on summer evenings.
The adults live for just a few
days and do not feed at all.

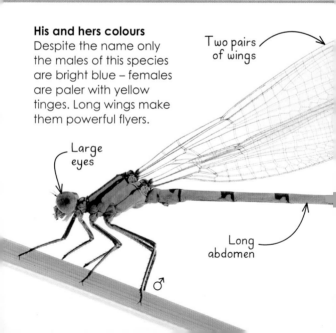

**His and hers colours**
Despite the name only
the males of this species
are bright blue – females
are paler with yellow
tinges. Long wings make
them powerful flyers.

Two pairs
of wings

Large
eyes

Long
abdomen

♂

**Wings and tails**
Unlike larger mayflies, this species has only two, rather than three, whip-like "tails". They also have only one pair of wings.

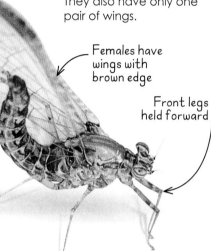

Females have wings with brown edge

Front legs held forward

Small ponds

Young eat algae

1.1 cm
(⅜ in)

# Common Blue Damselfly

Seen along the edges of rivers and ponds in summer, these insects hunt bugs living on the leaves of water plants.

Fresh water

Small insects

Dark stripes

*Seen it!*

3.5 cm
(1⅜ in)

### Spot the difference
Male and female hawkers look different. The males have bright blue marks on the long abdomen. Females have yellow spots.

Blue marks

Long abdomen ♂

Long, narrow wings

### Red or brown?
Seen between June and November, male darters have a red abdomen that ends in a point. Females are pale brown.

See-through wings

Huge eyes

♂

Red abdomen

# Common Hawker

These large dragonflies are always on the move, patrolling around ponds and grabbing other insects from the air.

**Seen it!**

Ponds, lakes, bogs

Flying insects

7.5 cm (3 in)

# Common Darter

This small dragonfly waits on twigs or fences for flying insects to pass before launching an attack. It is named after the way it makes short, fast flights as it chases prey.

Seen it!

Ponds, lakes, ditches

Insects

4 cm (1½ in)

### Speckled Bush Cricket

As in all crickets, the antennae
are as long as the body. This small,
noisy insect is found on rose
and raspberry bushes in late
summer and autumn.

Long antennae

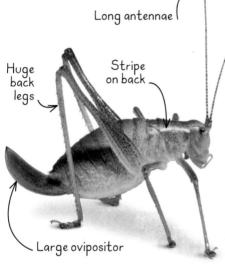

Huge
back
legs

Stripe
on back

**Seen it!**

Large ovipositor

### House Cricket

This cricket is originally from Asia
and Africa. It can be found feeding
on waste food and other rubbish on
warm summer nights.

**Seen it!**

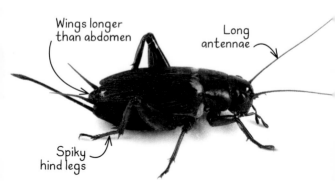

Wings longer
than abdomen

Long
antennae

Spiky
hind legs

## Common Field Grasshopper

Winged adults are a common sight in meadows in later summer and autumn. Before then you are more likely to come across the wingless nymphs.

**Seen it!**

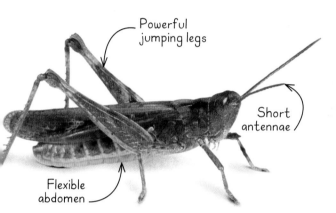

Powerful jumping legs

Short antennae

Flexible abdomen

## Meadow Grasshopper

This grasshopper's wings are shorter than its abdomen, and a female has smaller wings than a male. The adult male makes short clicking chirps.

**Seen it!**

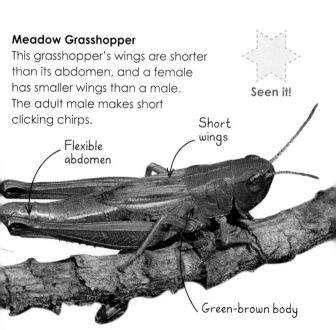

Short wings

Flexible abdomen

Green-brown body

# Wings and flight

Insects are the only type of bugs that can fly, but there are a lot of different types of insect, and they use their wings in many different ways.

### Wing structure

An insect wing is made from two thin layers of tough skin and is made stiff and strong by the blood-carrying veins running through it.

Tough, see-through wings

### Dragonfly

A dragonfly has four long, narrow wings, all about the same size. When it flies, the wings twist in circles instead of flapping up and down. This allows the dragonfly to fly very fast and to hover.

Hard wing case

### Beetle

The first pair of a beetle's wings is hardened into a wing case that opens to let the back wings out when the beetle flies.

Wings fold back

### House Fly

Flies only use two wings for flying. The second set have shrunk to very small rods, called halteres, that help keep the fly stable when it is flying.

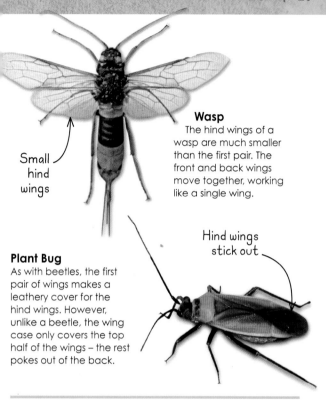

### Wasp
The hind wings of a wasp are much smaller than the first pair. The front and back wings move together, working like a single wing.

Small hind wings

### Plant Bug
As with beetles, the first pair of wings makes a leathery cover for the hind wings. However, unlike a beetle, the wing case only covers the top half of the wings – the rest pokes out of the back.

Hind wings stick out

### Ballooning
Although they cannot fly, small spiders move long distances by "ballooning" – letting out a few strands of silk that get caught by the wind and carry the spider away.

Silk produced by spinnerets on abdomen

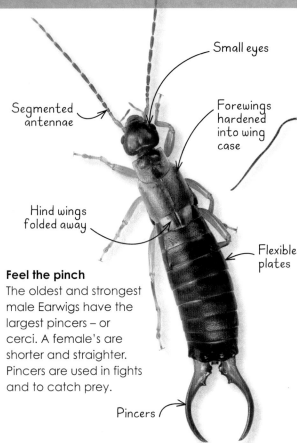

Small eyes

Forewings hardened into wing case

Segmented antennae

Hind wings folded away

Flexible plates

**Feel the pinch**
The oldest and strongest male Earwigs have the largest pincers – or cerci. A female's are shorter and straighter. Pincers are used in fights and to catch prey.

Pincers

# Earwig

These insects don't really crawl into human ears, but they do hide in warm, damp places during the day.

Forests, gardens

Fruits, flowers, small insects

1.5 cm (⅗ in)

Seen it!

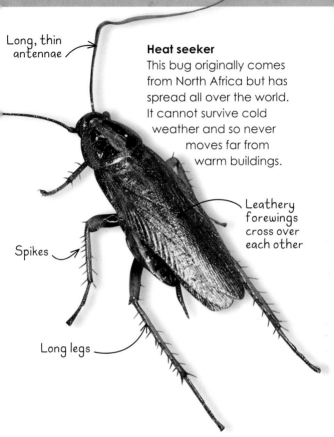

Long, thin antennae

**Heat seeker**
This bug originally comes from North Africa but has spread all over the world. It cannot survive cold weather and so never moves far from warm buildings.

Leathery forewings cross over each other

Spikes

Long legs

# Cockroach

Cockroaches avoid bright light and only come out in the dark. They scatter rapidly if disturbed.

Buildings, rubbish tips

Waste food

1.6 cm (⅝ inch)

seen it!

### Head Louse

This wingless insect lives on human heads, sucking blood from the scalp. Its eggs are called nits.

Short antennae

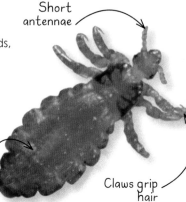

Flat body

Claws grip hair

Seen it!

### Cat Flea

Anyone with a pet cat – or dog – will meet this expert jumper at some point. They drink blood and will sometimes bite humans.

Hairy body

Small head

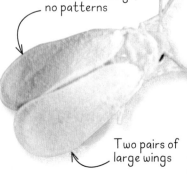

Long back legs used for jumping

Seen it!

### Greenhouse Whitefly

Commonly found in greenhouses and gardens, this tiny sap-sucking bug is most often seen as a wingless, wax-covered nymph.

Pure white wings, no patterns

Two pairs of large wings

Seen it!

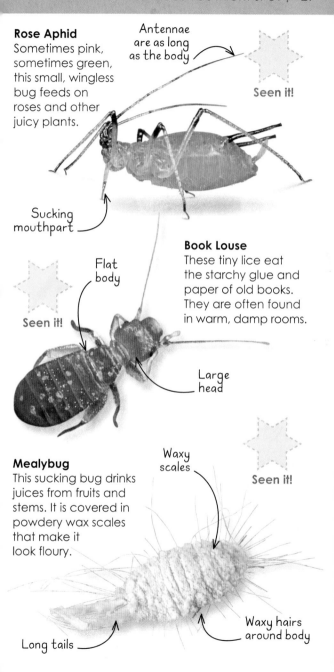

**Rose Aphid**
Sometimes pink, sometimes green, this small, wingless bug feeds on roses and other juicy plants.

Antennae are as long as the body

**Seen it!**

Sucking mouthpart

**Book Louse**
These tiny lice eat the starchy glue and paper of old books. They are often found in warm, damp rooms.

Flat body

**Seen it!**

Large head

**Mealybug**
This sucking bug drinks juices from fruits and stems. It is covered in powdery wax scales that make it look floury.

Waxy scales

**Seen it!**

Long tails

Waxy hairs around body

**Sap sucker**
This bug clings to the thinner stems of green plants, such as potatoes and gooseberries, and sucks out the sap.

Segmented antennae

Narrow body

Grey wing tips

# Common Green Capsid

The tiny nymphs of this bug appear in spring but the flying adults are most common in summer.

Gardens, fields, woods

Sap

7 mm (⅜ in)

seen it!

**Fruit feeder**
Stocky-bodied Forest Bugs suck juice from buds and fruit and also prey on smaller insects.

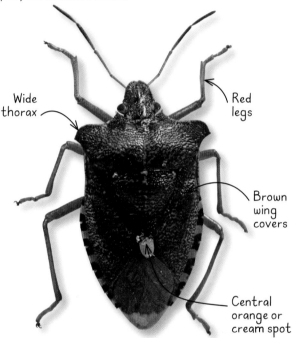

Wide thorax

Red legs

Brown wing covers

Central orange or cream spot

# Forest Bug

These bugs are seen on woody branches in summer and autumn, especially on fruit trees.

seen it!

Woodlands, orchards

Sap, fruit juices, insects

1.5 cm
(⅗ in)

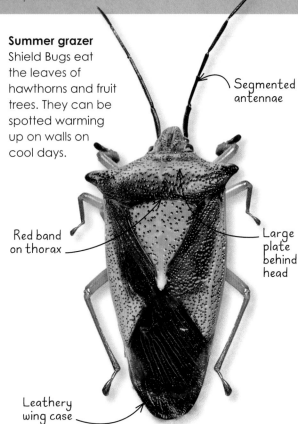

**Summer grazer**
Shield Bugs eat the leaves of hawthorns and fruit trees. They can be spotted warming up on walls on cool days.

Segmented antennae

Red band on thorax

Large plate behind head

Leathery wing case

# Shield Bug

Named after its shield-shaped body, this plant bug is seen in hedges and gardens between spring and autumn.

Shrubs, hedges

Leaves

1.5 cm (⅗ in)

**Seen it!**

**Sunbather**
The bugs are most often spotted on sunny summer days, clustered in groups on the ground near the bases of shrubs and trees.

Prominent eyes

Short wings

Black spots

Red wing case

# Fire Bug

Although rare in the UK, these bright red bugs can sometimes be seen searching the ground for seeds and insect prey.

Meadows, open gardens

Seeds, insects

1 cm (⅜ in)

**Seen it!**

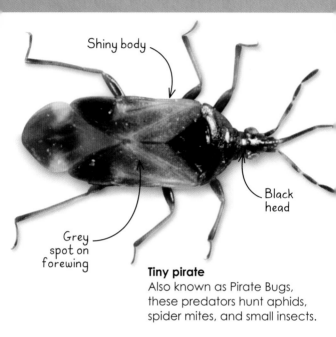

Shiny body

Black head

Grey spot on forewing

**Tiny pirate**
Also known as Pirate Bugs, these predators hunt aphids, spider mites, and small insects.

**In a lather**
The most obvious sign of froghoppers is cuckoo spit. This is the name for the nests of frothy bubbles the nymphs make to protect themselves.

Short antennae

Eyes on the sides of head

Wings held in tent shape

# Common Flower Bug

In winter these bugs hibernate in dead leaves and under bark. In summer they search for food on the leaves of shrubs and trees.

Woodlands, gardens

Insects, mites

4 mm (⅛ in)

**Seen it!**

# Common Froghopper

Adult froghoppers are good jumpers, as their name suggests, and they can also fly. They appear in gardens in late summer.

Garden shrubs

Plant sap

6 mm (¼ in)

**Seen it!**

# Noises

You can sometimes hear a bug long before you spot it. Some bugs make sounds to send messages to each other. Others are simply noisy.

### Scraping
Grasshoppers and crickets make short chirruping sounds by scraping their legs against their wings, or by rubbing their wings together.

Tymbals located under the wings

### Clicks
Cicadas are very noisy bugs. The males make loud calls by clicking flexible parts of the abdomen called tymbals. The bug uses its flying muscles to bend the tymbals, so they beat like a drum.

### Buzzing
Bees make a buzzing noise by flapping their wings very fast. This helps these big insects warm up their muscles so they can keep flying on cold days, which would be too chilly for other bugs.

### Whine

Mosquitoes fly in the dark, but you can hear the high-pitched whine they make. This is produced when they flap their wings super fast. The noise helps the little flies find each other so they can mate and lay eggs.

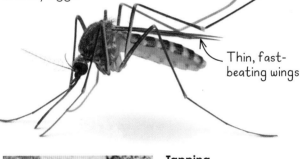

Thin, fast-beating wings

### Tapping

Wood-boring beetles spend most of their time out of sight in tunnels chewed through the wood. To find a mate, they tap their heads on the walls of the tunnel. If you are quiet, you can hear them tapping.

Breathing holes

### Hissing

The Hissing Cockroach makes loud hissing noises to scare off predators. It does this by squeezing air out of breathing holes along the side of its body.

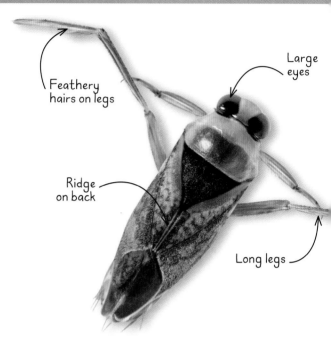

Feathery hairs on legs

Large eyes

Ridge on back

Long legs

**Rowing champion**
The Water Boatman rows along with its long back legs. The hairs on its body trap a supply of air bubbles so the bug can stay underwater for longer.

# Water Boatman

Also known as a Backswimmer, this bug swims upside down under the surface of ponds, hunting for prey.

Ponds, rivers

Tadpoles, small fish, insects

1.6 cm (⅝ in)

Seen it!

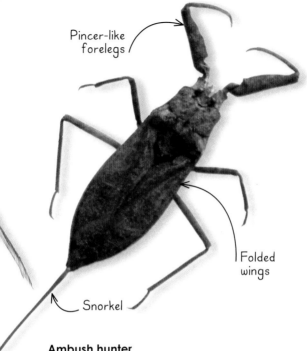

Pincer-like
forelegs

Folded
wings

Snorkel

**Ambush hunter**
The Water Scorpion hunts all year
round, grabbing prey with its strong
forelegs. It only flies when it needs
to find a new hunting ground.

# Water Scorpion

Despite its name, this insect is
more closely related to aphids. Its
long "stinger" is actually a snorkel
for breathing underwater.

Shallow
water

Insects, small
fish, tadpoles

2 cm
(¾ in)

Seen it!

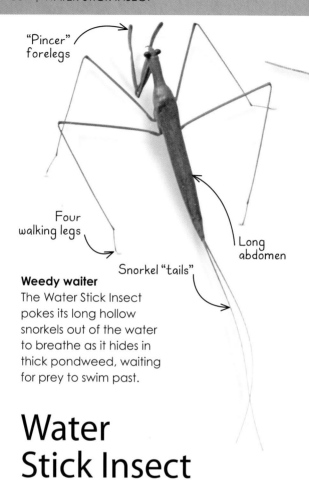

"Pincer" forelegs

Four walking legs

Snorkel "tails"

Long abdomen

**Weedy waiter**
The Water Stick Insect pokes its long hollow snorkels out of the water to breathe as it hides in thick pondweed, waiting for prey to swim past.

# Water Stick Insect

This lanky insect uses its twig-like disguise to creep up on prey before stabbing it with its sharp, beaky mouth.

Weedy, still water

Insects, fish, tadpoles

5 cm (2 in)

**Seen it!**

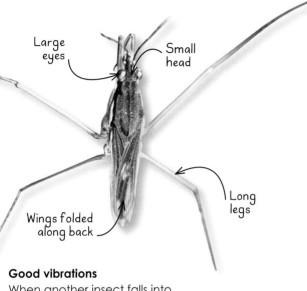

Large eyes

Small head

Long legs

Wings folded along back

**Good vibrations**
When another insect falls into the water, the Pond Skater picks up the vibrations through its feet, scuttles over to it, and grabs the prey with its front legs.

# Common Pond Skater

One of the easiest bugs to spot at ponds, this long, narrow insect is light enough to walk on top of the water.

Ponds, calm rivers

Insects

1 cm (⅜ in)

**Seen it!**

### Speckled sucker

This insect sucks sap from plants using its long, beak-like mouth. It is described as "tarnished" because of the dark speckles on its wing case.

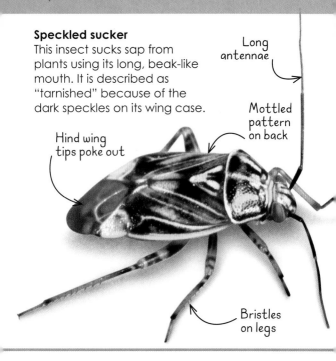

Long antennae

Mottled pattern on back

Hind wing tips poke out

Bristles on legs

### Storm warning

Thrips are also called Thunder Flies because they get swept up by strong winds and are only able to land again when the wind drops – often just before a heavy thunderstorm.

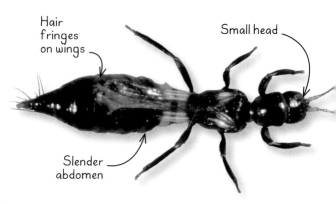

Hair fringes on wings

Small head

Slender abdomen

# Tarnished Plant Bug

You can spot this bug in late summer feeding on plants such as nettles, daisies, and clover in meadows. It is also a nuisance on potato farms.

Fields

Potatoes, other plants

6 mm (¼ in)

Seen it!

# Thrips

This very tiny insect has a flat body and small wings so it can wriggle right into the heart of a flower to feed on sap and pollen grains.

Shrubs, flowerbeds

Sap, pollen, mites

2.5 mm (⅛ in)

Seen it!

White spots

Clubbed antennae

Blue spots

Orange fringe

**Top and bottom**
The bottom of the dark wings,
seen when the butterfly rests,
have orange and blue marks.
The tops are orange and white.

# Red Admiral

One of the largest butterflies, this
species is often seen in autumn sipping
juice from fallen fruits and flowers.

**Seen *it!***

Woodland
fringes

Ivy, nettle
leaves

6 cm (2⅜ in)
wingspan

White spots on forewings

Brown-black wing tips

Hairy body

**Colourful wings**
In flight, the wings show orange patches. When perching, the folded wings are dull brown with dark blue spots.

Dark spots on hind wings

# Painted Lady

One of the most common butterflies, the Painted Lady flies in a spiralling path between wide, flat flowers.

*Seen it!*

Wild flowers

Nectar

5 cm (2 in) wingspan

**Codling Moth**
Caterpillars of this moth live inside apples and are often described as "apple maggots". The moth feeds on fruits and nuts.

Net-like pattern on wings

**Seen it!**

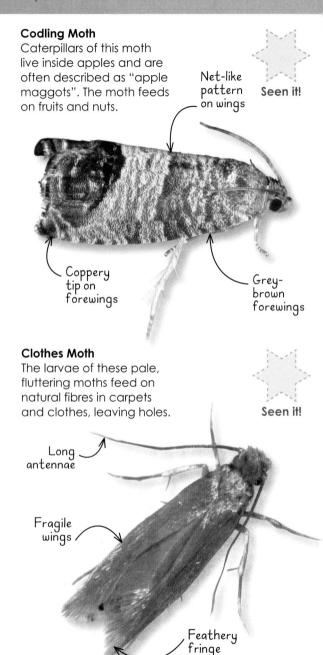

Coppery tip on forewings

Grey-brown forewings

**Clothes Moth**
The larvae of these pale, fluttering moths feed on natural fibres in carpets and clothes, leaving holes.

**Seen it!**

Long antennae

Fragile wings

Feathery fringe

## Large White

These butterflies feed on cabbages as caterpillars. The adults are seen in meadows and gardens on sunny days.

Seen it!

Black dots

Dark fringe

Dark body

White hind wings

## Poplar Admiral

One of the biggest butterflies in Europe, this species lives in forests and is especially common in places where aspen and poplar trees grow.

Seen it!

White marks

Dark wings

Blue and orange fringe

# Young bugs

Many of the bugs you find will not be the adults shown in this book. Instead they will be the young forms, such as caterpillars, maggots, or nymphs.

### Naiad

Dragonfly nymphs are called naiads. They live underwater and are fierce predators. The naiad only comes out of the water when it is time to change into an adult.

### Maggot

These worm-like fly larvae are usually found near rotting food. They seldom grow more than 1.5 cm (⅗ in) long.

Pale pink or yellow body

### Caterpillar

These are probably the most familiar young bugs. They are the larvae of moths and butterflies. Most of them live in bushes and trees, munching on the leaves.

Warning pattern to deter predators

### Grub

Young beetles are called grubs. They normally live buried in soil. The bigger beetle grubs grow slowly and can live underground for several years.

Spines at end of abdomen

Soft body

Head

### Spider sac

Many species of spider protect their eggs in a silken sac. You may see a female carrying one, or find one attached to the edge of a web.

### Hopper

A grasshopper nymph is sometimes called a hopper because it has no wings. All it can do is hop away from trouble.

### Cuckoo spit

This bubble mixture appears on the stems of certain plants in spring, when the cuckoos begin to call. The mixture is produced by froghopper nymphs, to protect them from predators.

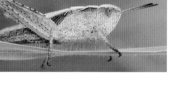

Froghopper nymph

Cuckoo spit

**Water babies**

Female Alderflies lay eggs on plants that hang above ponds and rivers. The larvae hatch out and fall into the water, where they become fierce hunters.

Wings held in tent shape

Long antennae

Dark body

**Night stalker**

Lacewings usually come out after dark. Both the adults and larvae feast on aphids that live on the smaller stems of bushes and trees.

Four wings

Golden eyes

Veins on see-through wings

# Alderfly

Adult Alderflies come out in early summer and become active around dusk. They do not feed and live just long enough to mate and lay eggs.

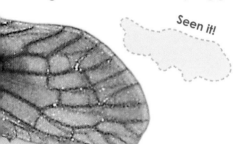

Seen it!

Riverbanks

Aquatic insects

1.2 cm (½ in)

# Green Lacewing

These delicate insects are weak flyers and are most often seen fluttering around lights at night.

Seen it!

Woods, hedges, gardens

Aphids

2 cm (¾ in)

# Scorpionfly

This insect is named after the unusual – and harmless – tip of the male's abdomen, which looks like a scorpion's sting.

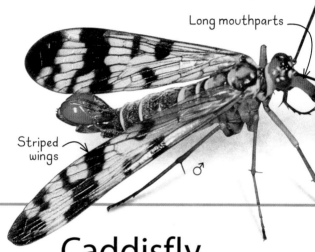

Long mouthparts

Striped wings

♂

# Caddisfly

Looking a bit like a moth, this insect is best seen perching on a stem with its wings folded upright. The adults live for only a few days.

Four wide wings

Long legs

## Hedgerow scavenger

Scorpionflies can fly but generally crawl around in shady hedgerows looking for dead insects and other food to scavenge.

Woodland, hedges

Dead insects

1.5 cm (⅗ in)

*Seen it!*

## Tough case

Caddisfly larvae live underwater inside a protective shell made from glued leaf and stone fragments.

Ponds

Long antennae

Filters food from water

3 cm (1¼ in)

*Seen it!*

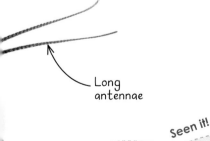

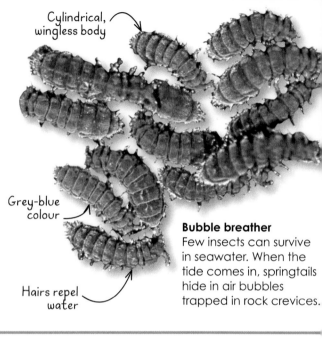

Cylindrical, wingless body

Grey-blue colour

Hairs repel water

**Bubble breather**
Few insects can survive in seawater. When the tide comes in, springtails hide in air bubbles trapped in rock crevices.

**Give them the slip**
This insect's body is covered in slippery silver scales. These allow the Silverfish to struggle free from predatory ants.

*Seen it!*

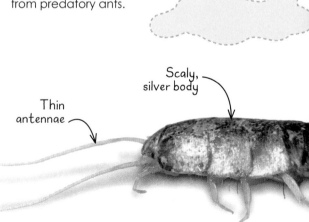

Scaly, silver body

Thin antennae

# Seashore Springtail

These tiny bugs float in clusters on the surface of still rockpools, or gather under the driftwood and rocks on the beach.

Tidal zone

Dead shellfish, seaweed

4 mm
(⅛ in)

Seen it!

# Silverfish

This wingless insect likes damp but warm places, such as kitchens and bathrooms. It can be hard to spot because it comes out at night and is a fast runner.

Houses

Crumbs, flour, paper

1.3 cm
(½ in)

Three "tails"

**Pond predator**

During the day this beetle hunts in clear, plant-filled ponds. At night it flies long distances to find new hunting grounds.

Air bubbles make body look silvery

Yellow fringe

Dark wing case

Large eyes

# Large Diving Beetle

One of the largest beetles in Europe, this pond insect paddles through water using its long, hairy back legs.

Ponds

Tadpoles, small fish, larvae

3.5 cm (1⅜ in)

Seen it!

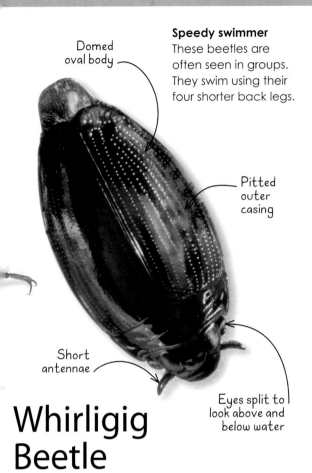

Domed oval body

**Speedy swimmer**
These beetles are often seen in groups. They swim using their four shorter back legs.

Pitted outer casing

Short antennae

Eyes split to look above and below water

# Whirligig Beetle

This shiny black species is named after the way it twists and turns on the surface of ponds before diving for cover.

Ponds

Insects

7 mm (⅜ in)

Seen it!

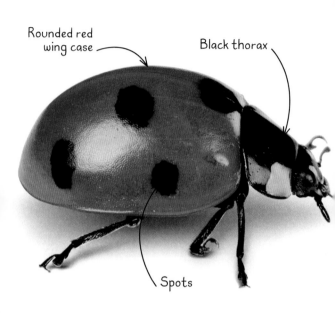

Rounded red wing case

Black thorax

Spots

Orangey-red wing case

Spots

Black eyes

Brown legs

# Seven-spotted Ladybird

This common ladybird species is seen between spring and autumn. In winter, the beetles hibernate in groups in dark places.

Gardens, meadows

Aphids

**More or less**
Normally red with seven black spots, these bugs can also be yellow or black with more or fewer spots.

**Seen it!**

8 mm
(³⁄₁₀ in)

# Harlequin Ladybird

This ladybird is originally from Asia but has been spreading across the world. It is most often seen on low-growing plants, such as nettles.

Woodlands

Aphids

**Pale alternative**
These beetles are a paler colour than European species and have more spots. Some are black with just four orange spots.

**Seen it!**

9 mm
(³⁄₁₀ in)

### Warning signal

When threatened, this beetle raises its abdomen as if to sting (it can't) and flashes its big, biting mouthparts. It can give a painful nip if handled carelessly.

Short wing case

Long abdomen

### Roving rotter

The Rove Beetle is a fierce hunter, always on the move as it searches through dead leaves for insect and mites. Its large mouthparts are perfect for killing prey and slicing up plants.

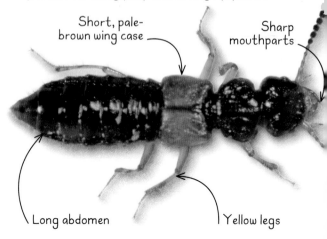

Short, pale-brown wing case

Sharp mouthparts

Long abdomen

Yellow legs

# Devil's Coach Horse

This large, dark-coloured relative of the Rove Beetle, is often seen hunting among piles of damp leaves and on flowerbeds.

**Seen it!**

— Knotty antennae

Damp leaves, soil

Slugs, insects

3 cm (1¼ in)

# Rove Beetle

At first glance this long, slender beetle is often mistaken for an ant. It is a fast runner, but has wings folded out of sight and is also a good flyer.

**Seen it!**

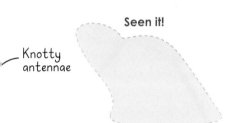

Compost heaps

Rotting plants, insects

6 mm (¼ in)

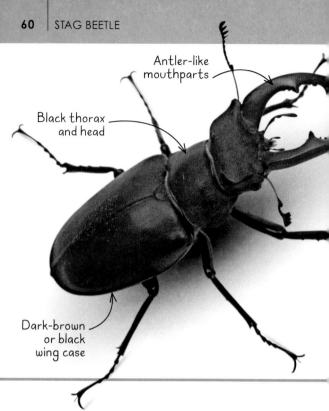

Antler-like
mouthparts

Black thorax
and head

Dark-brown
or black
wing case

**Fellow travellers**
The Dor Beetle is nicknamed
the Lousy Watchman because
it is often covered in mites.

Ridges on
wing case

Rounded
body

# Stag Beetle

The biggest beetles in the UK and Europe, Stag Beetles are named after the males' huge mouthparts, which look like antlers. They are used for fighting, not feeding.

Forests, parks

Tree sap

**Slow grower**
Adult Stag Beetles are common in dry, warm regions. They live only for a few weeks after spending up to seven years as a larva.

**Seen it!**

7.5 cm (3 in)

# Dor Beetle

This beetle spends its time under piles of animal dung, preparing a nest for its young, which feed on the poo. The best time to see one is on a warm summer evening.

Fields, gardens

Dung

Club-like antennae

**Seen it!**

2.5 cm (1 in)

**Striped critter**
This bug is also known as the Ten-striped Spearman due to its distinctive wing-case markings.

Bright yellow thorax with black spots

Wing case has ten stripes

Rounded body

# Colorado Potato Beetle

Originally from the USA, this small beetle and its larvae can wipe out potato, tomato, and aubergine crops.

Meadows, fields

Leaves

1.1 cm (⅜ in)

*seen it!*

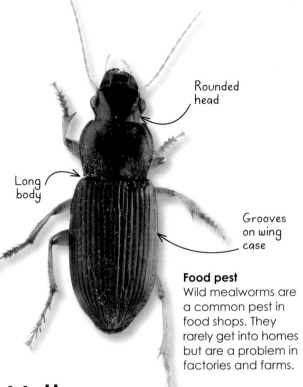

Rounded head

Long body

Grooves on wing case

**Food pest**
Wild mealworms are a common pest in food shops. They rarely get into homes but are a problem in factories and farms.

# Yellow Mealworm Beetle

As an adult, this beetle goes largely unnoticed. However, its grubs – known as mealworms – are often used as bait by anglers.

Seen it!

Food shops

Grains, flour, cereals

1.6 cm (⅝ in)

### Vine Weevil

These small, flightless beetles are a nuisance to gardeners worldwide. The grubs eat plant roots, while the adults munch holes in the leaves.

**Seen it!**

Ridges on back

Small head

Stubby snout

### Lesser Cloverleaf Weevil

These little beetles are found wherever clover grows. They are spotted between April and August, but bury themselves in the ground for winter.

**Seen it!**

Short hairs

Greenish-yellow markings

Pale stripes

### Grain Weevil

This weevil is also known as the "elephant bug" because it has a long trunk-like snout. It is actually a mouthpart for drilling holes in seeds.

**Seen it!**

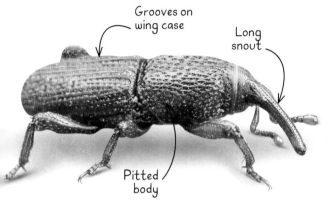

Grooves on wing case

Long snout

Pitted body

### Bark Beetle

Bark Beetle grubs burrow into tree trunks. Most live on dead wood and help break down old logs, but some attack and kill live trees.

**Seen it!**

Pits on wing cases

Hairy head and body

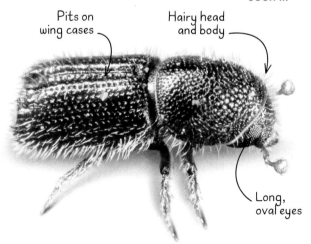

Long, oval eyes

**Fan feelers**

The male Cockchafer has huge fan-shaped antennae. The grubs live underground for three years after hatching, eating plant roots.

Fanned antennae

Rust-brown wing case

Pointed abdomen

# Cockchafer

A large beetle, the adult Cockchafer – or May Bug – can be found in early summer on shrubs and in trees.

Woodlands, gardens

Leaves, roots

3 cm (1¼ in)

**Seen it!**

**Spring return**

The adults hibernate under leaves in cold periods and come out again in spring.

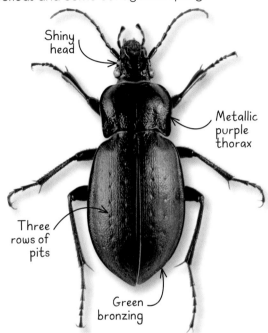

Shiny head

Metallic purple thorax

Three rows of pits

Green bronzing

# European Ground Beetle

This garden-friendly, caterpillar killer cannot fly, but clambers around in fallen leaves and soil looking for prey.

**Seen it!**

Gardens, woodlands

Caterpillars

2.5 cm (1 in)

# Green Tiger Beetle

This bright-green beetle is most common in grassy sand dunes and heaths, where its larvae make burrows.

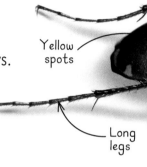

Yellow spots

Long legs

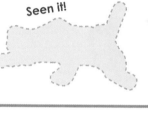

**Seen it!**

# Furniture Beetle

This beetle's grubs eat dead wood, burrowing into the trunks of fallen trees. But they also attack wooden furniture and can be seen in houses.

Short legs

**Seen it!**

## High-speed runner

The adult beetle is out and about in spring and summer. It is one of the fastest insects on six legs, chasing other insects over the ground.

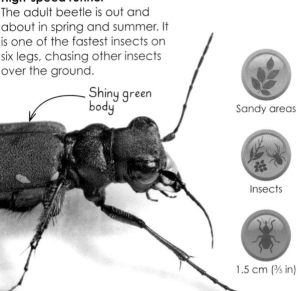

Shiny green body

Sandy areas

Insects

1.5 cm (⅗ in)

## Wood tunneller

The grubs, or woodworms, stay hidden from view. Sometimes the only sign you see is a tiny hole in the wood.

Clubbed antennae

Dead wood

Dead wood

5 mm (¼ in)

Helmet-shaped shield behind head

### Turf trouble

The adult beetle is seen buzzing around in early summer. The larvae, known as wireworms, feed on plant roots and can kill grassy lawns.

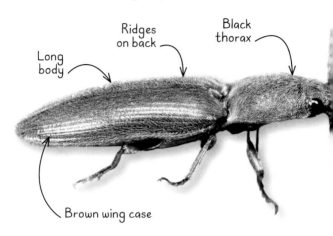

Long body

Ridges on back

Black thorax

Brown wing case

### Fiddly problem

Larder Beetles can turn up in houses. They even get into violin cases and eat the horse hairs making up the bow.

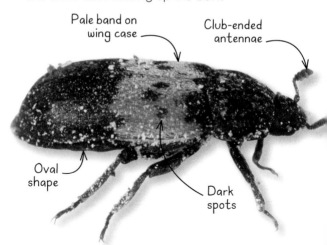

Pale band on wing case

Club-ended antennae

Oval shape

Dark spots

# Click Beetle

This beetle gets its name from the way it escapes if it is turned over by a predator. It bends its body so quickly that the insect flies into the air – with a loud click.

Grasses

Leaves, roots

1 cm (⅜ in)

Seen it!

# Larder Beetle

In the wild this beetle is found around the bodies of dead animals. Both the adults and larvae eat animal skin, hair, and feathers.

Bird's nests, houses

Dead animals, dried meat

1 cm (⅜ in)

Seen it!

### On parade
Old-fashioned British soldiers used to wear red uniforms, and the bright red patches on this insect have earned it the name Soldier Beetle.

Dark mark on thorax

Rectangular body

Black wing case

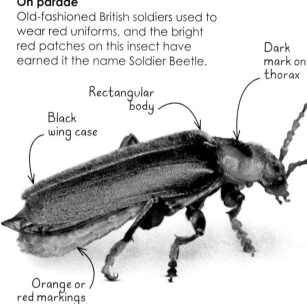

Orange or red markings

### Nobody's home
When disturbed, these beetles pull in their head and legs and lie still, pretending to be dead.

Head hidden under neck plate

Red and black wing case

Shiny body

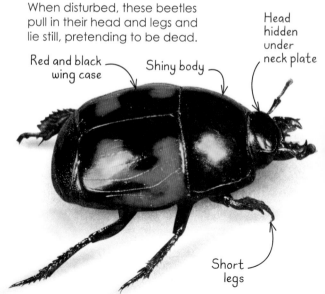

Short legs

# Soldier Beetle

This long beetle hunts in and around flowers between May and August. It is most common in damp but sunny habitats, such as the edges of woodlands.

Meadows, gardens

Small insects

1.4 cm (½ in)

Seen it!

# Hister Beetle

These small, rounded beetles are seen in late summer. The adults are fierce hunters and lay their eggs in dung or rotting animal waste for the larvae to eat.

Pastures, woodlands

Insect eggs, larvae

5 mm (¼ in)

Seen it!

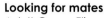

### Looking for mates
Adult Crane Flies do not
feed – they spend their
days searching for mates.
Their brown grubs are
known as leatherjackets.

Long legs

Two
wings

Halteres
(balance organs)

### Water insects
Mosquito larvae live in still,
stagnant pools. Adults are
common in late summer.

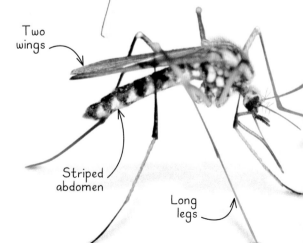

Two
wings

Striped
abdomen

Long
legs

# Crane Fly

A frequent visitor fluttering clumsily around homes in late summer and autumn, this gangly fly is perhaps better known as a Daddy Long-legs.

Seen it!

Grasslands, parks, gardens

Grubs eat plant roots

2.5 cm (1 in) body

# Mosquito

Although it does not spread diseases like some mosquitoes in other parts of the world, females of this little fly still bite humans to feed on blood.

Seen it!

Near stagnant water

Males: nectar Females: blood

6 mm (¼ in)

### Dance Fly
This hairy hunter snatches insects from flowers, pierces them with its long mouthpart, and sucks them dry.

**Seen it!**

Dark-grey body

Hairy legs

### Black Fly
This small bloodsucker lives in woods near water. Black Flies bite mammals, birds, and sometimes humans.

Mouthpart

**Seen it!**

Clear wings

Thick antennae

### Vinegar Fly
Also known as a Fruit Fly, this tiny insect flits around kitchens in summer, slurping up any oozing fruit juices.

**Seen it!**

Red eyes

Wings longer than abdomen

**Seen it!**

**Common Gnat**
Often mistaken for a Mosquito, this little fly rarely bites humans. It flies at night, giving out a low humming sound.

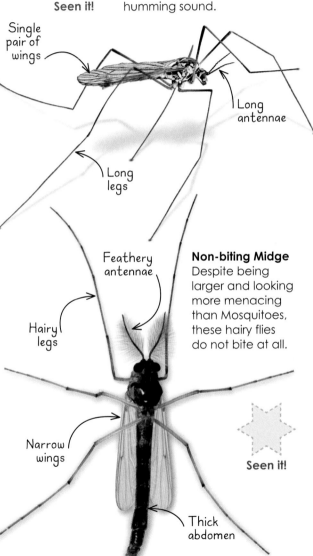

Single pair of wings

Long antennae

Long legs

Feathery antennae

**Non-biting Midge**
Despite being larger and looking more menacing than Mosquitoes, these hairy flies do not bite at all.

Hairy legs

Narrow wings

**Seen it!**

Thick abdomen

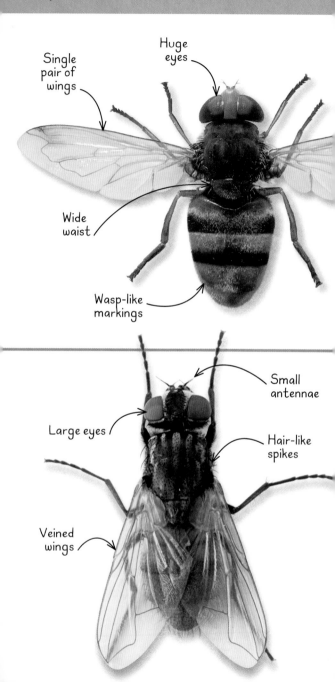

Single pair of wings

Huge eyes

Wide waist

Wasp-like markings

Small antennae

Large eyes

Hair-like spikes

Veined wings

# Hover Fly

With its stripy abdomen, this fly is often mistaken for a Wasp. The disguise fools predators, keeping them away while the Hover Fly feeds on nectar.

Gardens, parks

Nectar

**Slow flyer**
The Hover Fly is a better flier than a Wasp, and can be seen circling slowly around flower heads.

**Seen it!**

1.5 cm (⅗ in)

# House Fly

The larvae of this very familiar insect lie dormant in winter. When summer comes, the small adults buzz around areas with rubbish bins and waste food.

Houses

Waste food, dung

**Indoor acrobat**
House Flies are expert fliers, and can hover and fly backwards. Their hooked feet allow them to grip smooth surfaces.

**Seen it!**

8 mm (³⁄₁₀ in)

# Bug disguises

Some bugs are hard to spot because their colours help them blend in with their surroundings. Others are disguised to look like more dangerous bugs.

### Fooling the enemy

Predators are good at looking for bug-shaped things, so it helps if you can make them think you are something else. Stick insects have long, thin bodies that look like a twig, while other bugs are shaped like leaves or thorns.

Stick Insect

### Full camouflage

Some bugs blend in very well with their surroundings. Many have mottled patterns or splodges that disguise their shape and make them hard to spot. Others are coloured to match flowers or leaves.

Crab spider matches colour of petals

**Wasp**                    **Hover Fly**

### Warning signals

Stinging bugs show-off on purpose. The yellow stripes of a Wasp are a warning that it will sting if you get too close. Hover Flies cannot sting, but they have copied the Wasp's striped pattern to scare off attackers. Up close, a Hover Fly does not have a Wasp's narrow waist and it is a much slower flier.

### Scare tactics

Some camouflaged bugs keep a colourful pattern hidden from view under their wings, which they flash at predators to frighten them off. Butterflies and moths, such as this Emperor Moth, often have dark spots on their wings, which look like the eyes of a much bigger and scarier animal.

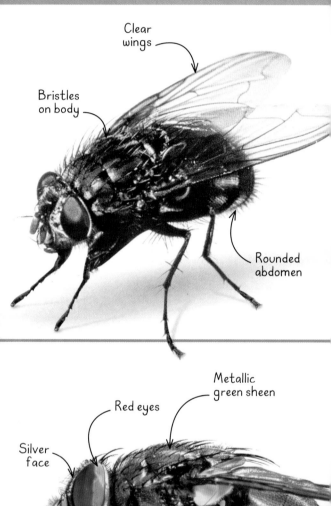

Clear wings

Bristles on body

Rounded abdomen

Metallic green sheen

Red eyes

Silver face

Hairy body

# Bluebottle

This big, buzzy fly is named after the metallic blue colour of its abdomen. Its legs and body are covered in stiff, bristly hairs.

Houses, gardens

**Mixed diet**
The female flies sniff out rotting meat to lay her eggs on, while the male feeds on flower nectar.

Rotting meat, nectar

*Seen it!*

1.5 cm
(⅗ in)

---

# Greenbottle

These bright, shiny green insects are slightly smaller than their blue cousins, and generally stay outside houses.

Gardens, parks, fields

**Meaty appetite**
After mating, the female flies lay their eggs on dead animals. The maggots hatch out and feed on the flesh.

Nectar, rotting meat

*Seen it!*

1.4 cm
(⅗ in)

**Male or female?**
It is easy to tell males from females
– the males are smaller, orange, and
don't have stripes or an ovipositor.

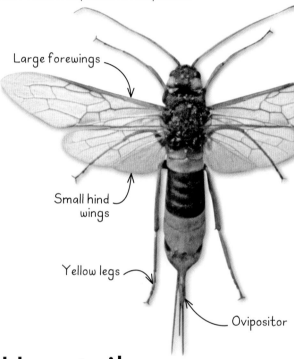

Large forewings

Small hind
wings

Yellow legs

Ovipositor

# Horntail

This large sawfly looks like a giant
wasp. However, the large ovipositor
is not a stinger, but is used
to lay eggs in bark.

Seen it!

Pine trees

Wood

5 cm
(2 in)

**Driller killer**

Females of this gangly insect use their long ovipositors to drill through tree bark into tunnels made by woodworms, where they lay their eggs. The larvae then eat the woodworms.

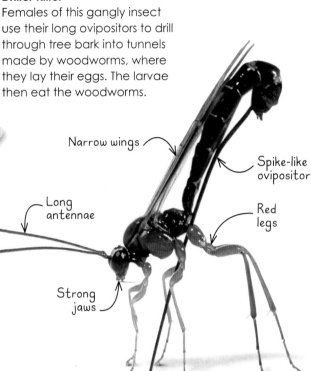

Narrow wings

Spike-like ovipositor

Long antennae

Red legs

Strong jaws

# Ichneumon Wasp

These scary-looking wasps are harmless to humans but are expert at detecting grubs hidden deep inside rotten wood.

Seen it!

Woodlands, hedgerows

Woodworms

3.5 cm
(1⅜ in)

### No sting in the tail
This species is harmless to humans
(most wasps cannot sting). They
are seen throughout the summer
looking for Mason Wasp nests.

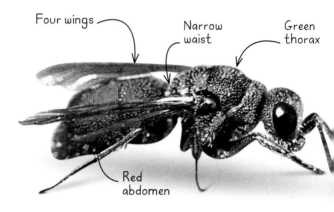

Four wings

Narrow
waist

Green
thorax

Red
abdomen

### Rotten nest
The Digger Wasp makes a nest by making
a hole in rotten wood or the pith of bamboo
canes. It then stocks it with aphids for its
larvae to eat when they hatch out.

Large
forewings

Square head

Hairy
body

Big
eyes

# Ruby-tailed Wasp

This colourful wasp is a parasite. Its larvae invade the nests of Mason Wasps inside tree trunks and crevices, and eat all the young.

Woodlands, gardens

Nectar

1 cm (⅜ in)

*Seen it!*

# Digger Wasp

Without the yellow and black stripes, this wasp looks more like a flying ant. The adults are active between May and September, while the young spend winter in the nest.

Gardens, forests

Aphids

1 cm (⅜ in)

*Seen it!*

**Danger sign**
The yellow stripes on the body serve as a warning that this insect stings when it feels trapped.

Bent antennae

Yellow stripes

Narrow waist

Long forewings

# Wasp

These stinging insects are very common in summer, when they buzz around collecting sugary foods from flowers and picnics.

Seen it!

Hedges, roofs, walls

Nectar, fruit juices

1.5 cm
(⅗ in)

**Hairy bee**
The thick layer of bristles makes this big insect look even larger. Even its tongue is hairy to help it suck up nectar.

Yellow band on thorax

Thick bristles

Stripy abdomen

# Bumblebee

These big buzzers are some of the first insects to appear in spring. They warm up in the cold by twitching their muscles.

Seen it!

Gardens, meadows

Nectar

2.2 cm (9⁄10 in)

### Busy worker

The faint stripes warn that Honeybees can sting, but they rarely do so. This bee is smaller than a Bumblebee and less colourful than a Wasp.

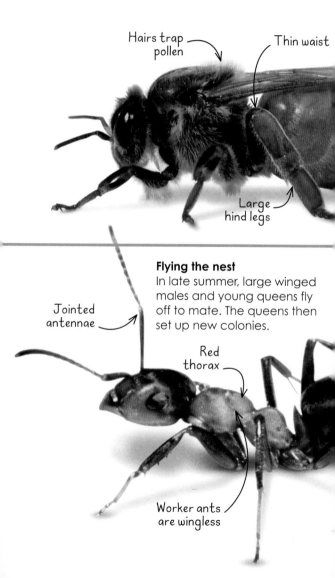

Hairs trap pollen

Thin waist

Large hind legs

### Flying the nest

In late summer, large winged males and young queens fly off to mate. The queens then set up new colonies.

Jointed antennae

Red thorax

Worker ants are wingless

# Honeybee

This insect is a common sight in flower-filled gardens in summer. It collects pollen and nectar, which is turned into honey back in the nest.

**Seen it!**

Nest in tree holes

Honey

1.5 cm
(⅗ in)

# Red Ant

Unlike most ants in Europe, red ants can give a painful, if harmless, sting. They live in underground nests and feed on scraps of dead animals.

*Seen it!*

Black abdomen

Meadows, gardens, parks

Rotting animals

Workers: 5 mm (¼ in)
Queen: 8 mm (⅜ in)

### Aphid herders

Black Garden Ants love honeydew,
the sugary waste made by aphids.
The ants guard the aphids and
stroke them to get a sweet drink.

Jointed
antennae

Narrow
waist

Black or dark
brown body

# Black Garden Ant

These common ants do not sting.
Their large underground nests
contain thousands of workers
but only one queen.

*Seen it!*

Gardens,
parks, fields

Nectar,
sugary foods

5 mm
(¼ in)

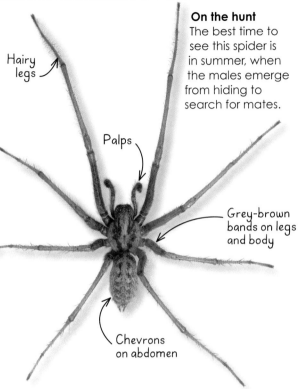

**On the hunt**
The best time to see this spider is in summer, when the males emerge from hiding to search for mates.

Hairy legs

Palps

Grey-brown bands on legs and body

Chevrons on abdomen

# Common House Spider

House Spiders are active all year around but spend a lot of time waiting for flying insects to hit their untidy cobwebs.

Houses, trees, caves

Insects

1.2 cm (½ in)

**Seen it!**

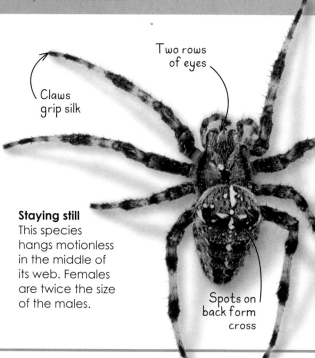

Claws
grip silk

Two rows
of eyes

**Staying still**
This species
hangs motionless
in the middle of
its web. Females
are twice the size
of the males.

Spots on
back form
cross

**Catching the breeze**
Money Spiders produce lines of silk from their
abdomens that catch the wind and carry
them off to new locations.

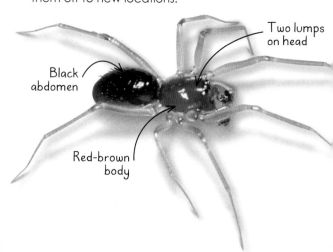

Two lumps
on head

Black
abdomen

Red-brown
body

# Garden Spider

This common spider is often seen on warm days in autumn when the large females, with eggs growing inside them, spin webs between plant stems.

Garden shrubs

Flying insects

Female: 1.8 cm (¾ in)

**Seen it!**

# Money Spider

These tiny spiders build small, horizontal, sheet-like webs in damp habitats between April and October. The spider waits under the web for an insect to become trapped.

Gardens, water meadows

Insects

3 mm (⅛ in)

**Seen it!**

# Webs

Many bugs use silk to wrap up food or line their nests. Spiders also use it to weave traps called webs that they use to snare other bugs for food.

**Silk moth**
The silk material that people wear comes from silk worms. Despite the name, these worms are actually caterpillars. The caterpillars spin the silk to make a protective cocoon (the yellow structures in the picture) while they change into a white moth. These cocoons are harvested and woven into fabric.

**Spinning a line**
Spiders produce silk from glands in the abdomen. Liquid silk is squeezed out and pulled into threads by tiny structures called spinnerets. The threads become solid soon after meeting the air.

## Weaving a web

The best web builders are the orb web spiders.
You can find them in most gardens in autumn,
when the females are feeding all day as they
grow eggs inside them. The spiders build a new
web every morning between plant stems.

### Step 1
The spider uses the wind
to blow the first thread
between two stems.

### Step 2
It spins another thread
and drops down to
make a Y shape.

### Step 3
More threads are strung
out from the centre.

### Step 4
The spider makes a
spiral of non-sticking silk.

### Step 5
The spider walks back
over the spiral and
replaces it with sticky silk
to trap prey. From then
on, it only walks on the
straight, non-sticky
"spokes" of the web.

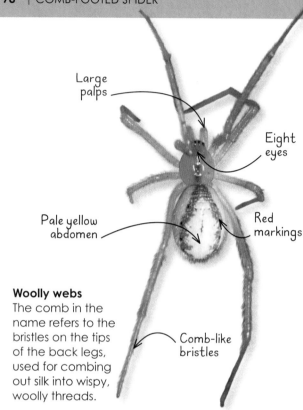

Large palps

Eight eyes

Pale yellow abdomen

Red markings

**Woolly webs**
The comb in the name refers to the bristles on the tips of the back legs, used for combing out silk into wispy, woolly threads.

Comb-like bristles

# Comb-footed Spider

After weaving a tangled web, the female spider builds a lair inside a curled leaf, in which she guards a large egg sac.

seen it!

Shrubs

Insects

7 mm
(⅜ in)

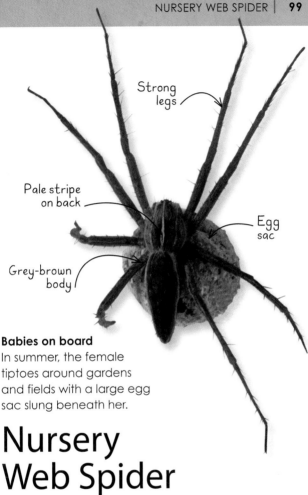

Strong legs

Pale stripe on back

Egg sac

Grey-brown body

**Babies on board**
In summer, the female tiptoes around gardens and fields with a large egg sac slung beneath her.

# Nursery Web Spider

This spider does not build a web to catch prey. Instead, females build tent-shaped "nursery webs" to protect their spiderlings.

Meadows, gardens, scrub

Ground insects

1.5 cm (⅗ in)

Seen it!

**Damp nests**
These spiders nest in damp outbuildings and
cellars. At the end of the summer, nests can
hold a mother and several biting spiderlings.

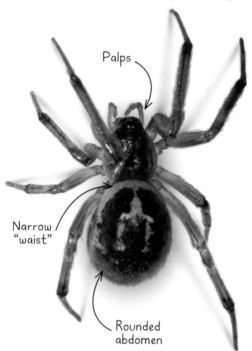

Palps

Narrow
"waist"

Rounded
abdomen

# Cellar Spider

One of the most venomous
spiders in Europe, this species
can give you a painful bite
if you disturb it.

Damp
hollows

Insects

8 mm
(⅜ in)

**Seen it!**

**Bungee jumper**
Jumping spiders stalk prey on walls and tree trunks. Before they pounce on their victim, they secure themselves with a silken safety line.

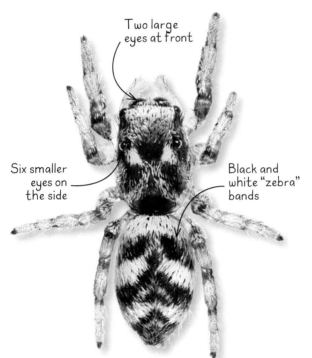

Two large eyes at front

Six smaller eyes on the side

Black and white "zebra" bands

# Zebra Spider

Although you may find it hard to spot this spider, it will probably see you first. All jumping spiders have very powerful eyesight.

Trees, walls, rocks

Insects, other spiders

6 mm (¼ in)

**Seen it!**

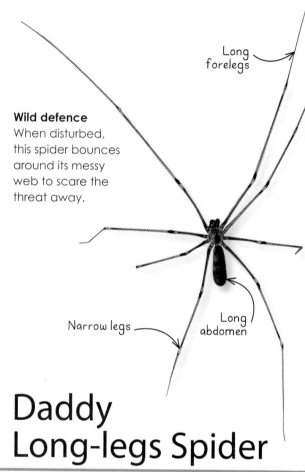

Long
forelegs

**Wild defence**
When disturbed,
this spider bounces
around its messy
web to scare the
threat away.

Narrow legs

Long
abdomen

# Daddy Long-legs Spider

This spindly species prefers dark, damp places and is common in cellars, but can also be seen crawling up walls in warm houses.

Damp, dark
places

Insects,
spiders

4 cm (1½ in)
legspan

Seen it!

**Chunky body**
The body has a single section with eight legs attached. The front pair of legs are used as feelers.

Extremely long legs

Eyes on stalks

Grey or brown body

Broad, rounded abdomen

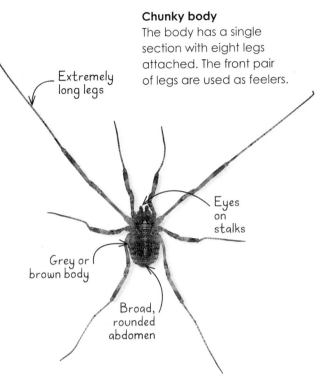

# Brown Harvestman

These long-legged relatives of spiders are mostly seen in the autumn, appearing at harvest time.

Seen it!

Woodlands, gardens

Small bugs

7 mm (⅜ in) body

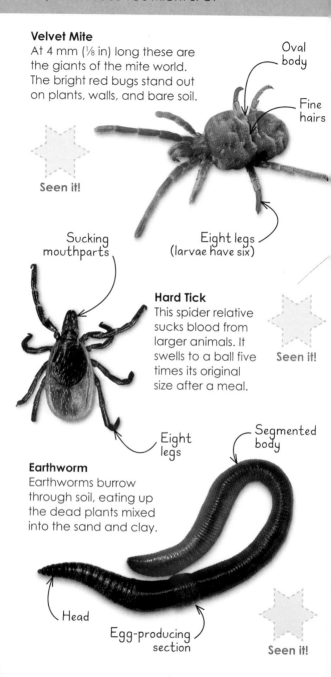

**Velvet Mite**
At 4 mm (⅛ in) long these are the giants of the mite world. The bright red bugs stand out on plants, walls, and bare soil.

Oval body

Fine hairs

Eight legs (larvae have six)

Seen it!

Sucking mouthparts

**Hard Tick**
This spider relative sucks blood from larger animals. It swells to a ball five times its original size after a meal.

Seen it!

Eight legs

Segmented body

**Earthworm**
Earthworms burrow through soil, eating up the dead plants mixed into the sand and clay.

Head

Egg-producing section

Seen it!

## House Centipede

Also known as the "moustache bug" because of its many long legs, this species is a hunter, preying on other household bugs.

**Seen it!**

One pair of legs per segment

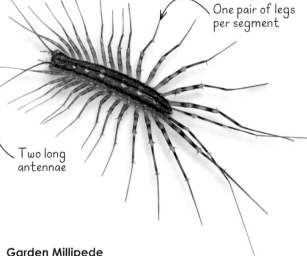

Two long antennae

## Garden Millipede

Also known as the Flat-backed Millipede, this species turns up in piles of dead leaves and under flat rocks, where it grazes on decaying plants and fungi.

Flat armoured plates on each segment

Two pairs of legs per body segment

Two antennae

**Seen it!**

# Pond Snail

These snails live in calm, freshwater ponds that are full of plants. They feed underwater but come to the surface to breathe.

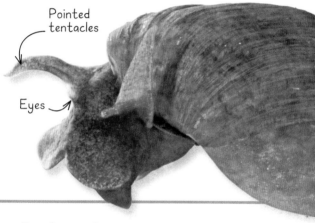

Pointed tentacles

Eyes

**Keeping cool**

Snails prefer wet conditions. When it is hot and dry, they find some shade and pull their shell down tight to keep themselves moist.

**Seen it!**

Hard shell

Slimy foot

**Touchy feelers**
Pond Snails have only two tentacles, while Garden Snails have four. Their eyes are at the base of the tentacles.

Seen it!

Ponds

Finely ridged surface

Long, pointed shell

Plants

1.5 cm (⅗ in)

# Garden Snail

A common sight in gardens, especially when crossing paths or exploring walls, this mollusc grazes on algae that grow on damp surfaces.

Gardens, woodlands

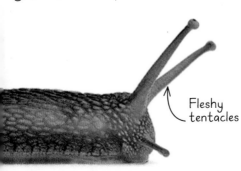

Fleshy tentacles

Algae, plants

4 cm (1½ in)

### Slimy coat

A slug has a tiny shell hidden inside its body. Slugs are covered in slime to stop them from drying out.

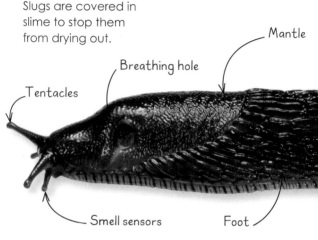

Mantle

Breathing hole

Tentacles

Smell sensors

Foot

### Cold and damp

Woodlice cannot survive far from water and live in cool, damp areas, such as under fallen leaves in flowerbeds.

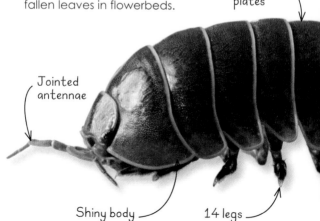

Flexible armoured plates

Jointed antennae

Shiny body

14 legs

# Slug

These large, soft-bodied molluscs are most often seen after rain, leaving silvery slime trails as they search for other slugs to mate with.

Skirt

*Seen it!*

Gardens, woodlands

Plants, fungus

8 cm
(3⅛ in)

# Woodlouse

This bug is not an insect or a spider, but a crustacean, a land-living relative of prawns and crabs. It is also known as a Slater, Sow Bug, or Pill Bug.

*Seen it!*

Loose soil, dead leaves

Dead plants

1.8 cm
(¾ in)

# Index

# Acknowledgments

**Dorling Kindersley** would like to thank: the staff of the RSPB, Louise Thomas for picture research, Tom Murray for supplying images, Sanjay Chauhan and Upasana Sharma for design assistance, and Anita Kakar and Ritu Mishra for additional editorial help.

The publisher would like to thank the following for their kind permission to reproduce their photographs:

(Key: a-above; b-below/bottom; c-centre; f-far; l-left; r-right; t-top)

**4 Corbis:** Visuals Unlimited (bl). **8 Alamy Images:** D. Hurst (tl); Igor Zhorov (cr). **Corbis:** Ken Wilson (bl). **9 Alamy Images:** Derek Croucher (tr); Victor Savushkin (br). **Getty Images:** Pier (c). **10 Alamy Images:** Ivan Andersen (tl); INSADCO Photography (cr); Nigel Cattlin (bl). **11 Getty Images:** Troup Dresser (b); Robert Pickett (cr). **12 Alamy Images:** (crb); Nigel Cattlin (cr). **Getty Images:** Anne Sorbes (clb); Tomatoskin (cl). **13 Dreamstime.com:** Peter Waters (cb). **FLPA:** Simon Litten (cr). **naturepl.com:** Kim Taylor (br). **14 Alamy Images:** Don Vail (bl). **Getty Images:** Bob Elsdale (cr). **18 Dorling Kindersley:** Courtesy of the Natural History Museum, London / Colin Keates (t). **Dreamstime.com:** Isselee (b). **23 Dorling Kindersley:** Courtesy of the Booth Museum of Natural History, Brighton / Dave King (tl). **Tom Murray:** (br, cr). **26 Science Photo Library:** James H. Robinson (b). **27 Corbis:** Visuals Unlimited (t). **Science Photo Library:** Courtesy Of Crown Copyright Fera (b). **32 Corbis:** Bert Pijs / Foto Natura (b). **34 Getty Images:** Hiroyuki Takeno (cr). **35 Alamy Images:** Manor Photography (cl). **Fotolia:** Andrew Burgess (b). **36 Fotolia:** Eric Isselée (c). **40 Alamy Images:** Nigel Cattlin (b). **Science Photo Library:** Science Source (t). **44 Corbis:** Nigel Cattlin (b). **Getty Images:** Visuals Unlimited, Inc. / Nigel Cattlin (t). **45 Corbis:** Volkmar Brockhaus (b). **46 Corbis:** David A. Northcott (tl). **47 FLPA:** Simon Litten (clb). **52 Alamy Images:** Blickwinkel (t). **62 Ardea:** John Mason (t). **63 Dreamstime.com:** (t). **64 Tom Murray:** (b). **65 Pavel Krásensky/ NaturePhoto.cz:** (t). **Tom Murray:** (b). **66 Alamy Images:** Juniors Bildarchiv GmbH (c). **Dreamstime.com. 67 Science Photo Library:** Barbara Strnadova (c). **69 Getty Images:** Nigel Cattlin (b). **70 Alamy Images:** Photoshot (t). **Corbis:** Nigel Cattlin (b). **72 Alamy Images:** Photoshot (t). **74 Getty Images:** Kunst & Scheidulin (b). **76 Science Photo Library:** Hermann Eisenbeiss (b). **Tom Murray:** (c). **77 Getty Images:** Nigel Cattlin (b); José Ramiro (t). **81 Alamy Images:** Naturepix (tr). **Getty Images:** Thomas Marent (cb). **82 naturepl.com:** Rolf Nussbaumer (b). **84 Dorling Kindersley:** Courtesy of the Booth Museum of Natural History, Brighton / Dave King (c). **86 Tom Murray:** (b). **92 Dreamstime.com. Getty Images:** Charles Krebs (c). **94 Tom Murray:** (b). **96 Alamy Images:** Eric Carr (bl). **Getty Images:** Inga Spence(c). **98 naturepl.com:** Kim Taylor (t). **100 Alamy Images:** Lee Dalton (c). **101 naturepl.com:** Alex Hyde (t). **104 Corbis:** Visuals Unlimited (c). **Science Photo Library:** Thomas Shahan (t). **105 FLPA:** Nigel Cattlin (b). **108 Dorling Kindersley:** Jerry Young (b)

**Jacket images:** Front: **Alamy Images:** Phil Degginger fcr; Spine: **Dorling Kindersley:** Courtesy of the Booth Museum of Natural History, Brighton / Dave King / ca

All other images © Dorling Kindersley
For further information see: www.dkimages.com

The author, **Tom Jackson**, has written and contributed to many books on animals and wildlife over the last 20 years. His love of nature has taken him on projects all around the world, from helping out in zoos to planting trees and animal conservation projects. He lives in Bristol, England, with his wife and three children.

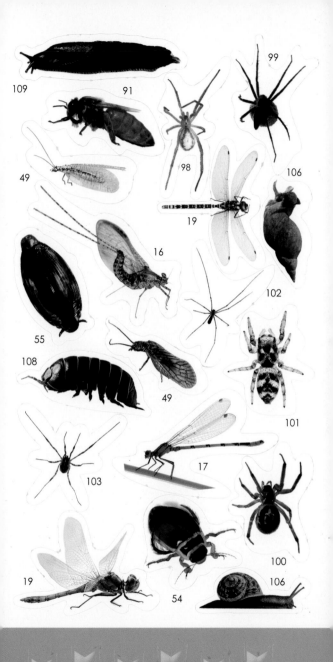

109

99

91

98

49

19

106

16

102

55

108

49

101

103

17

100

19

54

106

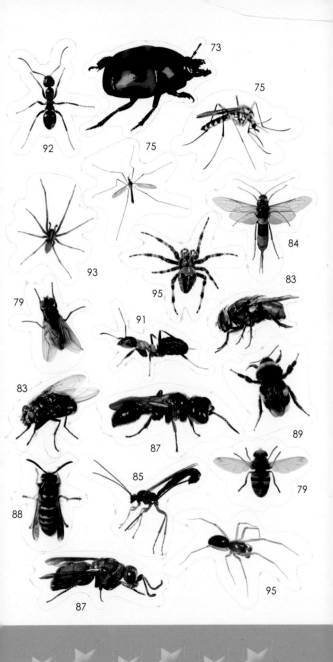

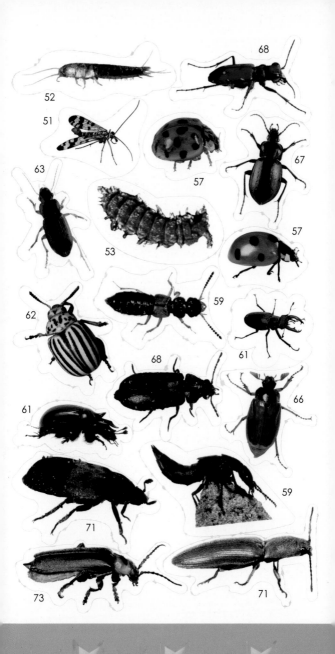